What's Inside an Ambulance?

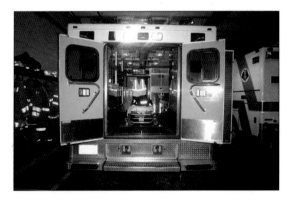

Sharon Gordon

*B*ENCHMARK *B*OOKS

NEW YORK

Inside an Ambulance

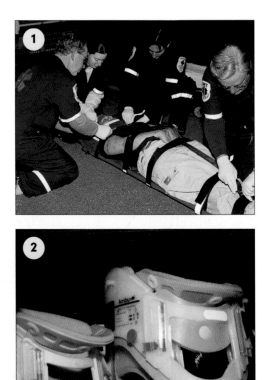

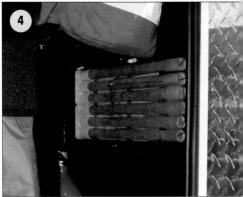

1. backboard
2. cervical collars
3. dressings
4. flares

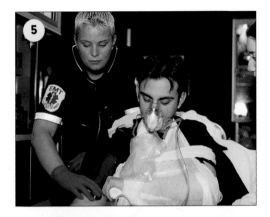

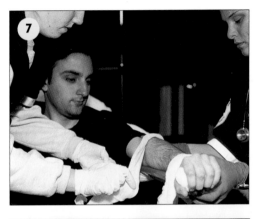

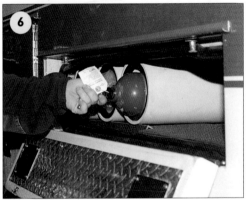

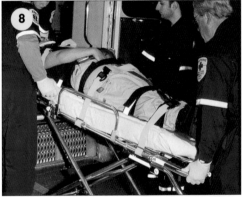

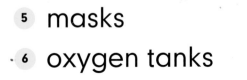

5 masks

7 splint

6 oxygen tanks

8 stretcher

3

Do you hear the loud *siren*?
Do you see the flashing lights?

The ambulance leaves the station in a hurry. Cars pull over and stop to let the ambulance pass.

Someone might be hurt or very sick.

The dispatcher calls for the ambulance. She tells the driver who needs help. She tells him what happened and where to go.

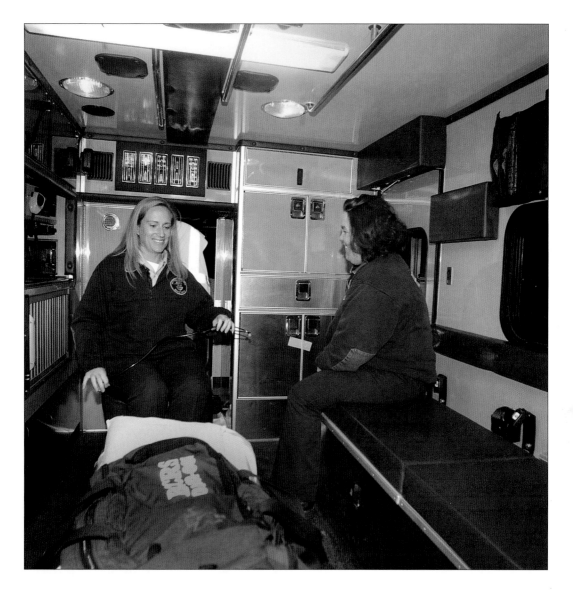

The workers inside the ambulance are called *emergency medical technicians*, or EMTs. They are trained for emergencies. They help sick and injured people.

Two EMTs sit in the front of the ambulance. The others ride in the back.

The shelves inside the ambulance are filled with medical supplies.

There are bandages of all sizes and shapes. There are *dressings* to put on cuts.

This front compartment has nighttime equipment. *Flares* light up the road and warn drivers. Vests glow in the dark for safety.

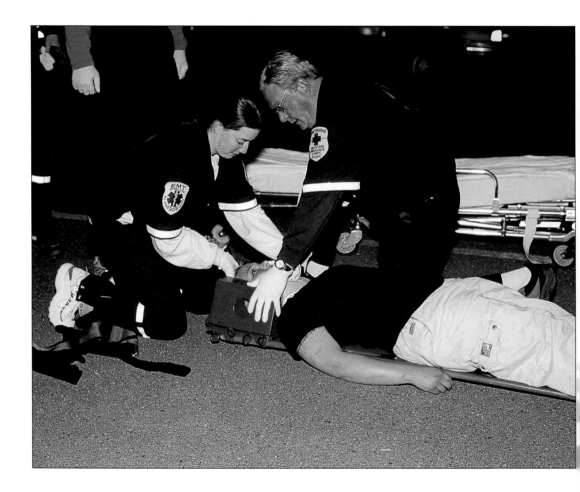

Sometimes the EMTs think there might be a serious injury. They must keep the person very still. Otherwise, the injury could get worse.

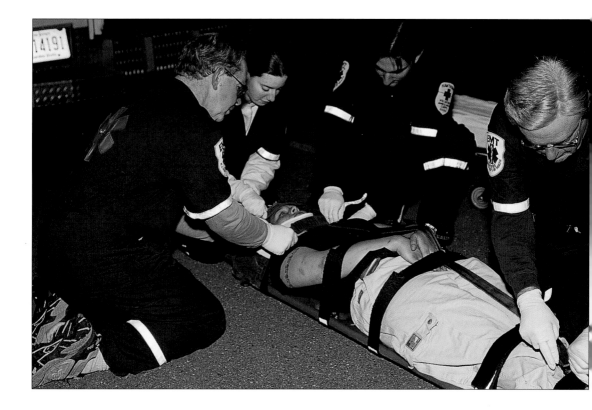

The EMTs may strap an injured person to a *backboard*. This stops the person's head, arms, and legs from moving.

They will also use a *cervical collar*. This keeps the person's neck still.

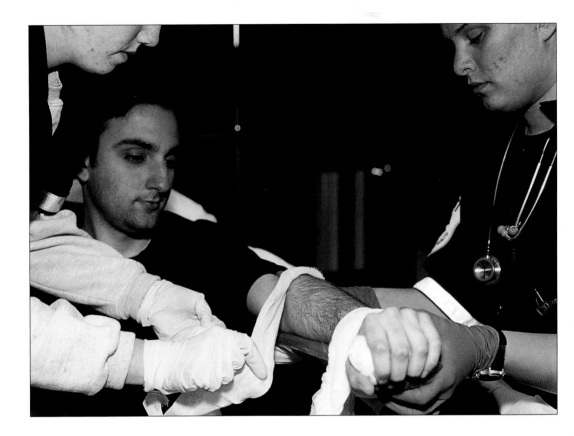

Sometimes the EMTs use a *splint*. It is for someone with a broken bone.

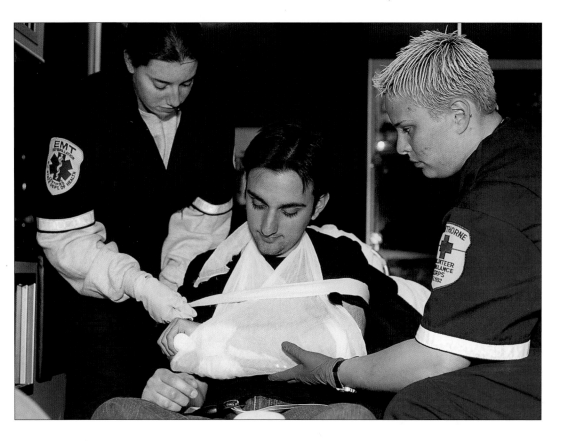

The splint keeps the person from moving the bone. This helps it hurt less.

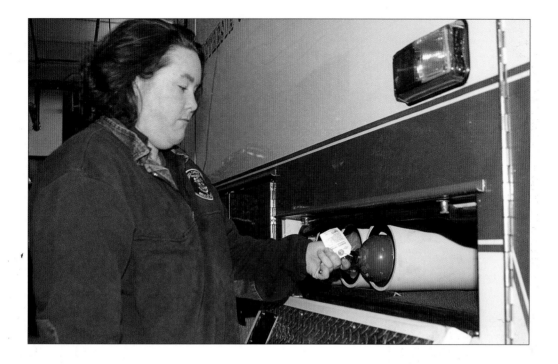

The oxygen compartment holds *oxygen tanks* and masks. The EMTs put a mask over the person's nose and mouth. This helps the person breathe.

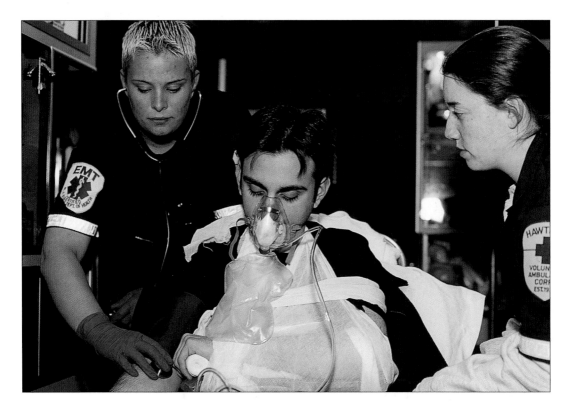

The EMTs listen to the heartbeat. They check the *pulse* and *blood pressure*.

The EMTs use the two-way radio to call the hospital. Workers in the emergency room get ready.

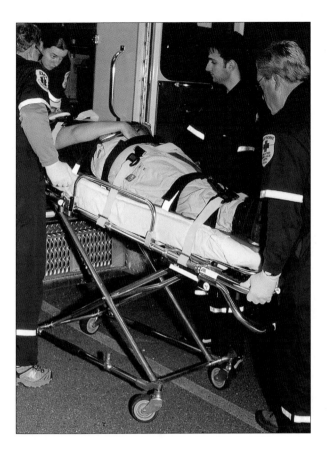

The person is carried in on a stretcher. A stretcher is a bed on wheels.

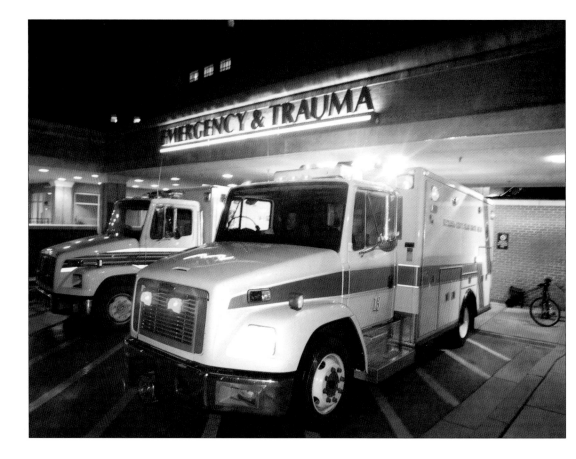

The emergency room doctors and nurses take over. They will find out what is wrong.

The ambulance leaves the hospital. The EMTs have done their job.

Inside the ambulance, the EMTs write down everything that happened. They return to the station.

The EMTs clean the ambulance and refill its supplies. It is ready for the next emergency in a flash!

Challenge Words

backboard—A hard board that keeps the back straight and still.

blood pressure—The pressure of the blood against the walls of the blood vessels.

cervical collar (ser-vi-kuhl collar)—A padded collar that keeps the neck still.

dressings—Bandages placed over a cut or sore.

emergency medical technicians (tek-ni-shuhns), EMTs—Rescue workers who care for injured people in an emergency.

flares—Bright warning lights.

oxygen tanks (ak-si-juhn tanks)—Tanks that store oxygen, a special gas that is needed to breathe.

pulse—The regular beating that is caused by the pumping movement of the heart.

siren (sigh-run)—An electrical horn that makes a loud up-and-down warning sound.

splint—A thin, stiff piece of wood, metal, or plastic that keeps a person from moving a broken bone.

Index

Page numbers in **boldface** are illustrations.

With thanks to Nanci Vargus, Ed.D.
and Beth Walker Gambro, reading consultants

ACKNOWLEDGMENTS
With thanks to the Bethesda-Chevy Chase Rescue Squad and the
Hawthorne Volunteer Ambulance Corps, Hawthorne, New Jersey

Benchmark Books
Marshall Cavendish
99 White Plains Road
Tarrytown, New York 10591-9001
www.marshallcavendish.com

Text copyright © 2004 by Marshall Cavendish Corporation

Library of Congress Cataloging-in-Publication Data

Gordon, Sharon.
What's inside an ambulance? / by Sharon Gordon.
p. cm. — (Bookworms: What's inside?)
Summary: Describes how the equipment on an ambulance is used on the way
to the hospital to help someone who is sick or hurt.
ISBN 0-7614-1561-0
1. Ambulance service—Juvenile literature. 2. Ambulances—Juvenile
literature. [1. Ambulance service. 2. Ambulances.] I. Title. II.
Series: Gordon, Sharon. Bookworms. What's inside?

RA995.G67 2003
616.02'5—dc21
2003005158

Photo Research by Anne Burns Images

Cover Photo by Jay Mallin

The photographs in this book are used with permission and through the courtesy of:
Jay Mallin: pp. 1, 2 (top right) (bottom), 3 (bottom left), 5, 6, 9, 10, 12, 13, 14, 22, 24, 26, 28, 29.
SWA Photography: pp. 2 (top left), 3 (top) (bottom right), 16, 18, 20, 21, 23, 25.

Series design by Becky Terhune

Printed in China
1 3 5 6 4 2